THE BLOOMING ORCHIDS

ENTERING INTO A POETIC WORLD.

ROHIT RAJ

This book is dedicated to my wonderful readers my family, friends and my teachers whom I admire the most.

Contents

Preface

As I bring out this book to you,I feel a sense of achivement.The Blooming Orchid benifits the every section of the society. It contain poems on different subjects written during different times . Through this book fellings of different types of people are expressed.This book can change the life and thinking pattern of peoples . This book conveys the different types of problems faced by several people such as a wonam , a soldier,a freedom fighter etc. No one can understand each other problems unless it falls upon you.

Acknowledgements

I would like to acknowledge and give my warmest thanks to my family members and my teachers who made this work possible. Their guidance and advice carried me through all the stages of this book. I would like to thank my committee members for providing me with the brilliant suggestion for my poems.

I would like to give special thanks to my teacher Sir Samir Biswas for making me aware with my talent and helping me in the edting of this beautiful book.. Your supports substain me far.

Finally I would like to thank god for letting me through all the difficulties.I have experienced your guidance day by day. You are the one who let me finish my first book and I am looking forward for writing much more .

Once again thank you all and Love you all.

1. Behind the poems

<u>**1. Journey of a Woman**</u>

Journey of a woman makes us aware about the sacrifices that a woman made as she grows from child to adult .How her responsibility increses as he enters her next stage of life. Women are equally important in society as men are. They are the backbone for a progressing nation. Demographically, half a population of the country constitutes women, and they deserve equal importance and rights in society.Besides managing household works, women should engage themselves in the service sector like banks, hospitals, airlines, schools and every other possible work field as well as they should start showing interest in setting up their own business. Not to mention, they are providing excellent outcomes in their respective areas. In the world of sports, women have set up milestones for men to achieve.
In this poem three stages of a girl life is explained. The first one is when she is someones daugher,fulfilling her duties towards her parents.Next comes when she is someone wife carriying on her duties towards her new family and life. The third stage in her life is when she becomes a mother making her child to be responsible ,and have to make the future bright

<u>2. The Wounded Soldier.</u>

A soldier has many duties to perform. He has to work selflessly for the betterment of the country. They ensure that peace and harmony are maintained throughout the nation. Moreover, they also remain vigilant at all times and render help in case of emergency situations.Almost all of the year, soldiers are on call. It is necessary for them to be away from their family and friends during this time. As a soldier, this is one of the most challenging aspects. It can be emotionally distressing.As a soldier, the first and foremost duty is to serve their country. The country's citizens sleep peacefully when their soldiers perform their duties genuinely.

In this poem The Wounded Soldier we hear a story of wounded soldier in a battle field.Soldiers are the pride of our country. They are ready to give sacrifice of their lives any time to protect the country. The life of a soldier is very uncertain. This poem tells how a soldier gave up his for his motherland leaving all his responsibility towards his family and friends behind.

3. The Voice of The Soul.

Life is concerned about the vital air inside our body. Death results when the vital air escapes from the body.Life means the state of living. Death means the state of being dead.The soul is the most precious part of the human because it is more important than life itself. Every living human being shares the same characteristic as other human beings by possessing a soul. The soul is even a labeled characteristic of people who have already died. The soul stays with a person for all of eternity. It is something that is grown with a person as they move through life.

The purpose of life is to be able to grow your own soul
The Voice of a Soul tells an unknown feeling of a soul a he left a body.How the soul feel seeing himself lying dead.He has many things to say wants to hug his near and dear ones but could as he was non more alive. This poem speak in the voice of a soul who wishes to convey many things.

4. The Turban Man

March 23, 1931, will be forever etched on the minds of Indians, as on this day 3 young revolutionaries of the Indian National Movement were hanged till death. Bhagat Singh, Sukhdev, and Rajguru were convicted for their involvement in the assassination of assistant superintendent of police John Saunders. The poem The Turban Man deals with the revolutionary man Bhagat Singh and his friends. They put the heart and soul to fight againts British. Though they die at a young age but had succeded in bringing a revolutionary. Bhagat Singh Sukhdev and Rajguru were indeed a true patriot. Not only they fought for the freedom of the country but also had no qualms giving away his life in the event. Their death brought high patriotic emotions throughout the country. Their followers considered them a martyr. We still remember him as a true freedom fighter.

5.An Unforgetttable Massacre

Jallianwalla, also called Massacre of Amritsar, incident on April 13, 1919, in which British troops fired on a large crowd of unarmed Indians in an open space known as the Jallianwala Bagh in Amritsar in the Punjab region of India, killing several hundred people and wounding many hundreds more. The incident showed the behavior of the British officers towards the Indians. It showed the wild side of the British. They constituted by an oppressive ideology of the British government that was ruling over India.

The poem An Unforgettable Massacre depits the cruel beheavior of the British government .he crowd gathered at Jallianwala Bagh consisted of unarmed men, women, and children. It was the festival of Baishakhi, and there was a fair. Many visitors had gathered at this fair. The British General Dyer got the news, and he ordered his troops to shoot indiscriminately at the gathering. There was one working exit at Jallianwala Bagh, which was blocked out by the General. Hundreds of innocent people lost their lives in this Massacre..

6. The Seed.

Growing up into a mature adult is a journey we all have to go through at one point in our life. For some, maturity came quicker with past experiences that mold us into who we are. For myself, maturity came quicker than anticipated because the absence of adulthood. What made me the independent young woman I am today is my life journey. Today we will talk about the journey of a seed. Seed Germination Seed germination is the process in which seeds or spores sprout and begin to grow after being dormant for a period of time. The length of dormancy varies depending environmental conditions in which the seed is surrounded by. The environmental conditions that determine when a seed will begin to germinate are the temperature, oxygen, the amount of light, and the supply of water

In this poem the joirney of a seed to plant is very well explained. How he grew himselg from a seedling to plant .Burried deep into the soil fighting for sunlight and water. Blooming inspite of heavy sunlight and even in harsh wheather condition.

7. *On a Snowy Night.*

In this poem we came across a couple who is out for a walk on a snoey night. How this romantic enviroment filling love in the air. The walk on a snowy night where they promises to be together no matter its heaven or hell. On a Snowy Night is the story of a writer passing through the streets on a snowy night. The writer of the poem is traveling in the dark through the snow with his beloved wife.

The writer says in his life he want to do many things enjoy many moments with his beloved wife. The love, affection, care and kindness are the true virtues of life. The concept of love with humans, with community and with all living beings is the essence of life The love is very important element of life where his love is made only for his beloved wife.

8. My Unknown Lover.

People often talk about love, but most of us are not fully aware about its true essence. There is lot of misconception about efficacy of love that holds us back to generate loving feelings towards others.Romantic love is a form of love that is often regarded as different from mere needs driven by lust. Romantic love generally involves a mix of emotional and soul wit inner feelings.
Love is not possessiveness. People look love as a possession that has to be acquired and preserved. To expect that others ought to provide it to us so that our life is filled with love is the biggest fallacy, which is cause of much unhappiness.
In this poem the poet describe the lover which he doesnt want to reaveal to the world. He lover her unconditionaly and classify his love a true love .Love is a set of emotions and behaviors characterized by intimacy, passion, and commitment. It involves care, closeness, protectiveness, attraction, affection, and trust.

• 9 •

<u>*Entering into a Poetic World*</u>

Lets begin with the journey.

2. Journey of a Woman

Journey of a woman,
is not an easy one.
Changing its goal of life,
as the new person enters by.
Sometimes to be someone's daughter,
making your parents feel prouder.
For your rights you must fight,
should do always what is right.
Sometimes to be someone's wife ,
commence your new family and life .
No matter how ill were you treated,
go ahead burying your dignity in entombed.
Sometimes to be someone's mother,
making sure your child doesn't suffer.
Guiding them with love and affection,
to become a man with perferction.

3. The Wounded Soldier

The intense battle was going on,
when a soldier was hit by one.
Someone's brother or Someone's son,
was down with a heart pierced one.
The pain of the soldier was increasing by,
then he saw his friend near by .
He calls his friend in a low voice,
who didn't hear even called twice.
The soldier soon gave up his life ,
thinking of his mother and married wife.
How will they live their rest of the life ,
without him in the world full of strife.
Who will share my beloved sorrow,
who will wipe her tears tomorrow.
Who will whisper the words of cheer,
when she will sat down with tears.

4. The Voice of the Soul

My soul left my body,
leaving everyone behind.
Family ,friend even my beloved,
couldn't hear me now, Why?
All were sitting around me,
Sheding their tears upon.
I wanted to wipe of their tears,
but I couldn't , Why?
Death took me away,
though my soul was near by.
I could see them all:
but they cannot, Why?
My body lie down there,
without a soul inside by,
My beloved shook me and cry ,
mother sitting beside and staring by .
Before leaving this mighty world ,
I wanted to hug them and cry,
Though my last wish was ,
that I could say a final Goodbye.

5. The Turban Man

A man with a turban ,
and a moustache on his face
Just of twenty three of age ,
was with a revolutionary image.
He fought for our freedom,
with a selfless attitude.
Though he was caught ,
by the British troop.
He along with his two friend ,
were supposed to be hanged.
But even at his tough time,
had not given up his pride.
The intense battle for independence ,
ended with British suspension,
Our love for you three will never fade ,
India reached where you wished to take.

6. An Unforgetable Massacre

The day was pleasant and a charming one,
people gathered to celebrate a festive one.
Together with happiness and joy ,
they came to celebrate and rejoice.
As the clock struk five on thirteen April,
the sweetness in the air was no longer avail.
The atmosphere was no longer familiar,
feeling of uncertainity was more near.
The devil dyer soon reached there ,
with a cruel plan seems to be fear.
Along with his troop at the entry gate,
shot down everyone of holy fate.
The soil changes its colour to red ,
To be the remembrance of the bad fortune we had.
O countrymen dont forget this day of blood,
do shed tears and remember them once.

7. The Seed

This is the seed,
which I plant with care.
Gviving it water,
to sprout it my dear.
As comes the seedling out ,
head held high with proud.
The petals of the seedilng was seen,
My little plant colour was green.
It grew as he promised,
so strong and tall ,
He try to be the best he can,
and didn't give up at all.
Standing straight upright,
Inspite of heavy sunlight.
Bearing buds and fruits,
blooming in heavy sunlight.

8. On a Snowy Night.

Journey on a snowy night,
together with my beloved wife.
Holding each other hands,
walking on a snowy land.
Looking in each other eyes,
promises which we could follow by.
Will love each other well,
no matter if its heaven or hell.
I offer you my love with purity,
and promises to bring happiness and security.
No matter how harsh the life become,
will hold each other hand one more time.

9. My Unknown Lover.

Loves the way you look at me ,
showering back the smile which I give.
No matter how I be ,
everytime you resemble me.
The white dress which I wear,
you are ready with same adorn,
Sometimes I think how alike we are ,
on this Earth in an heavenly hour.
Your eyes resembles mine ,
though we are both twenty nine.
In this false world my dear ,
Our love must be example to hear.
My friends must be eager to see,
how my love of the life be .
Her name you want hear,
Let her be an unknown dear.

End

I would like to give special thanks to my readers for readig "The Blooming Orchids". This was my small attempt towards my goal. Therefore I want to sincerely and officially thank you for the time you have given in reading this book. I promise to bring much more books in near fuure.

Thank you....

www.ingramcontent.com/pod-product-compliance
Lightning Source LLC
Chambersburg PA
CBHW021815150726
47989CB00004B/1936